PARDONED

**PRAYERS
& PROMISES FOR
PRISONERS**

John M. Robertson

TYNDALE HOUSE
PUBLISHERS, INC.
WHEATON, ILLINOIS

The interior artwork in this book was drawn by resident artists of Cook County Department of Corrections. Tyndale House wishes to thank them and also to acknowledge the cooperation of Chaplain Steven Thompson and Merritt P. Marks, Cook County art instructor, for making the project possible.

All Bible quotations are from *The Living Bible* and are used by permission.

First printing, September 1983

Library of Congress Catalog Card Number 83-50074
ISBN 0-8423-4831-X, paper
Copyright © 1983 by John M. Robertson
All rights reserved
Printed in the United States of America

PREFACE

For those
  who are imprisoned
    by themselves
    by their sins
    by their society;
For those
  who are looking
    for new hope
    for new freedom
    for new life;
May God
  speak to them
    in their condition
    through the words
    of his Living Word
And in Christ
  may they realize
  they are
    "ransomed, healed,
    restored, forgiven."

jmr

ALONE

The cell door
  has slammed shut
    behind me.
O God,
  I am alone—
    alone to bear
      the consequences
    of my crime.
I don't know if
  I can stand it, Lord,
    facing a future
      behind prison walls;
    being separated from
      my family and friends;
    living with others
      whose wills have
        been broken,
      whose hearts have
        become hardened,
      whose feelings have
        become empty.
Lord,
  I know I don't
    deserve it but
  I need all the help
    you can give me.

How I plead with God, how I implore his mercy, pouring out my troubles before him. For I am overwhelmed and desperate, and you alone know which way I ought to turn to miss the traps my enemies have set for me. (There's one—just over there to the right!) No one gives me a passing thought. No one will help me; no one cares a bit what happens to me. Then I prayed to Jehovah. "Lord," I pled, "you are my only place of refuge. Only you can keep me safe.

"Hear my cry, for I am very low. Rescue me from my persecutors, for they are too strong for me. Bring me out of prison, so that I can thank you. The godly will rejoice with me for all your help." *Psalm 142*

O Jehovah, how long will you be angry with us? Forever? Will your jealousy burn till every hope is gone? . . . Oh, do not hold us guilty for our former sins! Let your tenderhearted mercies meet our needs, for we are brought low to the dust. Help us, God of our salvation! Help us for the honor of your name. Oh, save us and forgive our sins. . . . Listen to the sighing of the prisoners and those condemned to die. Demonstrate the greatness of your power by saving them. *Psalm 79:5, 8, 9, 11*

GUILT

My guilt
  weighs heavy
    on me, Lord.
Some call it
  misbehavior;
    others say it is a
  wrongdoing;
    the courts call it a
  crime.
But Lord,
  your Word calls it a
    sin
And today
  I would confess
    my crime as a
      sin.
I have broken
  your commandments,
    I have forsaken
  your laws;
    I stand guilty before you and
  your righteousness.
Lord,
  there is nothing
    I can do to take away
  this guilt feeling.
Help me!

As the Scriptures say,
"No one is good—no one in all the world is innocent."

No one has ever really followed God's paths, or even truly wanted to.

Every one has turned away; all have gone wrong. No one anywhere has kept on doing what is right; no one....

Wherever they go they leave misery and trouble behind them, and they have never known what it is to feel secure or enjoy God's blessing.

They care nothing about God nor what he thinks of them.

...not one of them has any excuse; in fact, all the world stands hushed and guilty before Almighty God. *Romans 3:10-12, 16-18, 19b*

O Lord, from the depths of despair I cry for your help: "Hear me! Answer! Help me!"

Lord, if you keep in mind our sins then who can ever get an answer to his prayers? But you forgive! What an awesome thing this is! That is why I wait expectantly, trusting God to help, for he has promised. *Psalm 130:1-5*

FEAR

O God, I live in fear—
in fear of my own safety
and the awful things
that can happen here;
in fear of the guards
and their dislike
and personal threats;
in fear of other prisoners
and what they
might do to me;
in fear for my family
and what might be
happening to them.
Lord, I have no one
to turn to;
no one cares;
no one listens.
Lord,
the future seems
dark and forboding;
I weep and tremble
as I sit alone
being afraid.
Stay close
to me, God;
watch over me
and protect me.

Fear not, for I am with you. Do not be dismayed. I am your God. I will strengthen you; I will help you; I will uphold you with my victorious right hand. *Isaiah 41:10*

Shall I look to the mountain gods for help? No! My help is from Jehovah who made the mountains! And the heavens too! He will never let me stumble, slip or fall. For he is always watching, never sleeping. *Psalm 121:1-4*

Even when walking through the dark valley of death I will not be afraid, for you are close beside me, guarding, guiding all the way. *Psalm 23:4*

He will take care of the helpless and poor when they cry to him; for they have no one else to defend them. He feels pity for the weak and needy, and will rescue them. He will save them from oppression and from violence, for their lives are precious to him. *Psalm 72:12-14*

LONELINESS

I feel forsaken
  in this place, Lord—
    abandoned by my
      friends and acquaintances,
There seems to be
  no one who really cares
    or understands my
      feelings and anxieties.
I am lonely, God,
  I need someone
    who will care,
    who will be concerned,
    who will communicate.
O God,
  don't abandon me
    to an empty existence,
    to a life empty
      of relationships.
I am lonely
  and alone!
Lord, be
  my companion,
  my counselor,
  my comforter.

Lord, hear my prayer! Listen to my plea!

Don't turn away from me in this time of my distress. Bend down your ear and give me speedy answers, . . . I lie awake, lonely as a solitary sparrow on the roof. *Psalm 102: 1, 2, 7*

Jehovah himself is caring for you! He is your defender. He protects you day and night. He keeps you from all evil, and preserves your life. He keeps his eye upon you as you come and go, and always guards you. *Psalm 121:5-8*

If you love me, obey me; and I will ask the Father and he will give you another Comforter, and he will never leave you. He is the Holy Spirit, the Spirit who leads into all truth. The world at large cannot receive him, for it isn't looking for him and doesn't recognize him. But you do, for he lives with you now and some day shall be in you. *John 14:15-17*

HATRED

I hate today, Lord.
  I hate this place!
  I hate the warden!
  I hate the guards!
  I hate the inmates!
I know
  hatred is wrong
    and can only lead
      to greater pain
      and frustration.
But it's a feeling
  I can't get rid of, Lord.
But then
  I don't know
    if I want to.
It gives me
  an excuse
    to be angry and
      to strike back.
And yet, Lord,
  I know this is
    not your way.
Take away
  this hurt and hatred.
Give me
  your peace
    in my heart.

A hot-tempered man starts fights and gets into all kinds of trouble.

Pride ends in a fall, while humility brings honor.

A man who assists a thief must really hate himself! For he knows the consequence but does it anyway.

Fear of man is a dangerous trap, but to trust in God means safety.

Do you want justice? Don't fawn on the judge, but ask the Lord for it!

The good hate the badness of the wicked. The wicked hate the goodness of the good. *Proverbs 29:22-27*

There is a saying, "Love your *friends* and hate your enemies." But I say: Love your *enemies!* Pray for those who *persecute* you! In that way you will be acting as true sons of your Father in heaven. *Matthew 5:43-45a*

I am leaving you with a gift—peace of mind and heart! And the peace I give isn't fragile like the peace the world gives. So don't be troubled or afraid. *John 14:27*

WORRY

O God,
  I can't help wondering
    about my family;
  I can't help being worried
    over their welfare:
      Are they all right?
      Who's taking care of them?
      Where are they
        spending their time?
      How are the kids
        doing in school?
      Do they have enough money
        to meet their needs;
        to pay the bills?
O Lord,
  while I am
    locked up in this place,
I am helpless
  to help them.
Take care of
  my loved-ones, Lord.
Let them know that
  I love them
    and miss them
      and care about them.

Let him have all your worries and cares, for he is always thinking about you and watching everything that concerns you. *1 Peter 5:7*

Give your burdens to the Lord. He will carry them. He will not permit the godly to slip or fall. *Psalm 55:22*

Don't worry about anything; instead, pray about everything; tell God your needs and don't forget to thank him for his answers. If you do this you will experience God's peace, which is far more wonderful than the human mind can understand. His peace will keep your thoughts and your hearts quiet and at rest as you trust in Christ Jesus.... And it is he who will supply all your needs from his riches in glory, because of what Christ Jesus has done for us. *Philippians 4:6, 7, 19*

THE CHAPLAIN

I feel uneasy
  around him, Lord.
Is it because
  he represents you
    and your righteousness?
Is it because
  he disturbs my conscience
    and only adds to my guilt?
And yet he is
  your servant, Lord.
    When I gripe,
      he understands;
    when I complain,
      he serves;
    when I hurt,
      he helps.
I know I'm not always
  pleasant to him
    and yet I expect
      him to be
  pleasant to me.
Help me, God,
  to remember that
    he is doing his best
  to make me feel
    at my best.
Thank you, Lord,
  for having him care.

Dear brothers, I am not writing out a new rule for you to obey, for it is an old one you have always had, right from the start. You have heard it all before. Yet it is always new, and works for you just as it did for Christ; and as we obey this commandment, *to love one another,* the darkness in our lives disappears and the new light of life in Christ shines in. *1 John 2:7, 8*

For I know the plans I have for you, says the Lord. They are plans for good and not for evil, to give you a future and a hope. In those days when you pray, I will listen. You will find me when you seek me, if you look for me in earnest. *Jeremiah 29:11-13*

Jesus said to them, "You are truly my disciples if you live as I tell you to, and you will know the truth, and the truth will set you free." *John 8:31, 32*

CHAPEL

The stillness
　of a sanctuary—
The peacefulness
　of the prison chapel!
It's a great place
　to be with you, God;
To sit in silence
　To whisper my deepest needs
　　To tell you how I feel
　　　To thank you for your love
　To listen for your voice
　　To know that I don't have
　　　to face my troubles alone.
The assurance
　and reassurance
　　that comes from
Your Word
　and the hymns—
I need this, Lord.
　Thank you
　　for being here;
　　thank you
　　　for your promise
　　　　to be with me
　　　　at all times.

Come, kneel before the Lord our Maker, for he is our God. We are his sheep and he is our Shepherd. Oh, that you would hear him calling you today and come to him! *Psalm 95:6, 7*

Pray all the time. Ask God for anything in line with the Holy Spirit's wishes. Plead with him, reminding him of your needs, and keep praying earnestly for all Christians everywhere. *Ephesians 6:18*

The one thing I want from God, the thing I seek most of all, is the privilege of meditating in his Temple, living in his presence every day of my life, delighting in his incomparable perfections and glory. There I'll be when troubles come. He will hide me. He will set me on a high rock out of reach of all my enemies. Then I will bring him sacrifices and sing his praises with much joy. Listen to my pleading, Lord! Be merciful and send the help I need. *Psalm 27:4-7*

ENEMIES

O God,
  in this place it seems
    that one is surrounded
      by enemies.
There seems to be
  no one you can trust,
  no one you can depend on,
  no one you can turn to.
Everyone wants
  to take advantage of you,
  to use you for their own ends,
  to manipulate your life
    for their selfish purposes.
O God,
  I need to be delivered
    from threats,
    from being man-handled,
    from physical abuse,
    from mental anguish.
Deliver me, I pray—
  deliver me from
    the taunts and threats,
    the frustrations and fears,
    the abuse and aggravations.
Deliver me, O God,
  from the hands
    of my enemies.

Lord, you are my refuge! Don't let me down! Save me from my enemies, for you are just! Rescue me! Bend down your ear and listen to my plea and save me. Be to me a great protecting Rock, where I am always welcome, safe from all attacks. For you have issued the order to save me. Rescue me, O God, from these unjust and cruel men. O Lord, you alone are my hope....
Psalm 71:1-5a

Come quickly, Lord, and answer me, for my depression deepens; don't turn away from me or I shall die. Let me see your kindness to me in the morning, for I am trusting you. Show me where to walk, for my prayer is sincere. Save me from my enemies, O Lord, I run to you to hide me. Help me to do your will, for you are my God. Lead me in good paths, for your Spirit is good.
Psalm 143:7-10

If someone mistreats you because you are a Christian, don't curse him; pray that God will bless him. *Romans 12:14*

Yes, and the Lord will always deliver me from all evil and will bring me into his heavenly kingdom. To God be the glory forever and ever. Amen.
2 Timothy 4:18

FRIENDS

I found some
   friends today, Lord;
      people I could
         identify with,
         be honest with,
         share my life with.
And, Lord,
   I believe the feelings
      were mutual;
   they were willing
      to relate to me.
So many times
   we just need
   someone
      to talk to,
      to listen to;
   someone who
      understands and
      shows some compassion.
Today, you made
   that possible, Lord.
Help me to build
   on those relationships
      and to be the kind
   of friend
      they are looking for.

There are "friends" who pretend to be friends, but there is a friend who sticks closer than a brother. *Proverbs 18:24*

A true friend is always loyal, and a brother is born to help in time of need. *Proverbs 17:17*

Don't just pretend that you love others: really love them. Hate what is wrong. Stand on the side of the good. Love each other with brotherly affection and take delight in honoring each other....
  When others are happy, be happy with them. If they are sad, share their sorrow. Work happily together. Don't try to act big. Don't try to get into the good graces of important people, but enjoy the company of ordinary folks. And don't think you know it all! *Romans 12:9, 10, 15, 16*

VISITORS

What can I say
   to visitors, Lord?
I'm almost
   too embarrassed
      to see them.
Words will not
   come easily;
      there will be
   forced smiles and
      friendly greetings.
But can we
   go beyond
      mere chit-chat?
Can I share
   my hurt and helplessness;
      my fears and frustrations;
         my grief and guilt?
O Lord,
   at a time like this
      I need those who will
         take time to visit.
Help me
   to be honest
      with them;
   to let them know
      I appreciate their
         caring and concern.

Continue to love each other with true brotherly love. Don't forget to be kind to strangers, for some who have done this have entertained angels without realizing it! *Hebrews 13:1, 2*

But now the Lord who created you, O Israel, says, Don't be afraid, for I have ransomed you; I have called you by name, you are mine. When you go through deep waters and great trouble, I will be with you. When you go through rivers of difficulty, you will not drown! When you walk through the fire of oppression, you will not be burned up—the flames will not consume you. For I am the Lord your God, your Savior, the Holy One of Israel.... *Isaiah 43:1-3a*

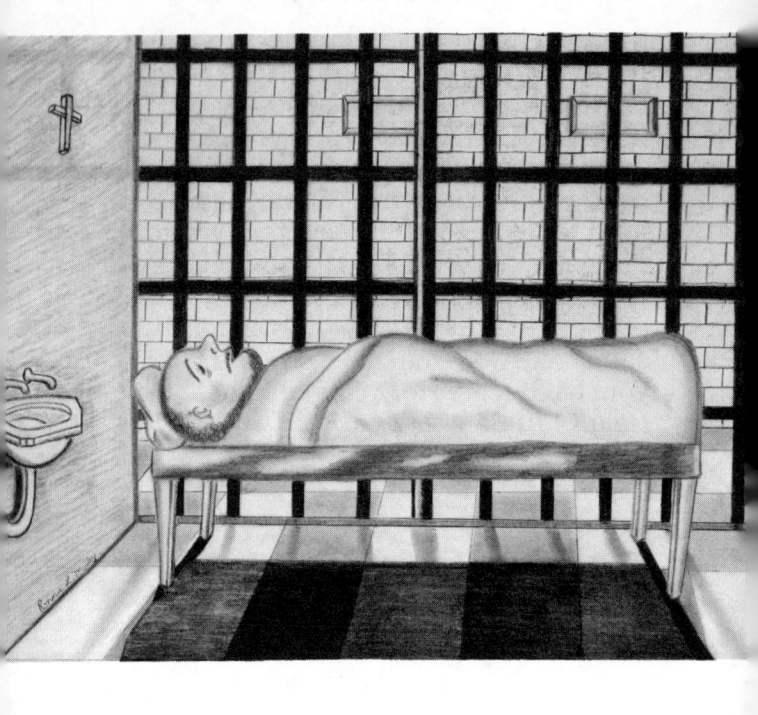

SICKNESS

O Lord,
  I don't feel
    very well today.
My body
  seems to be sapped
    of its energy.
I feel weak
  and nauseated
    and feverish.
But Lord,
  I don't want to be
    checked out by a doctor;
  I don't want to be
    examined and probed,
      fed pills or medicine;
  I don't want to be
    given shots.
Help me, God,
  to feel better
    to regain my strength
      to be back on my feet.
But help me, too,
  to be thankful
    for my health.

For the Lord God, the Holy One of Israel, says: Only in returning to me and waiting for me will you be saved; in quietness and confidence is your strength;... *Isaiah 30:15*

Happy are those who are strong in the Lord, who want above all else to follow your steps.... They will grow constantly in strength and each of them is invited to meet with the Lord in Zion. *Psalm 84:5, 7*

But they that wait upon the Lord shall renew their strength. They shall mount up with wings like eagles; they shall run and not be weary; they shall walk and not faint. *Isaiah 40:31*

Always give thanks for everything to our God and Father in the name of our Lord Jesus Christ. *Ephesians 5:20*

DESPAIR

Despair has hit me, God.
  All sense of caring
    has gone from me.
Disappointment
  Discouragement
    Disillusionment
      rule the day.
I want to
  hit!
    move!
      strike!
      run!
But I can't!
  I'm locked
    in this cell!
O God!
  Help me—
    Help me
      to see
      to sense
        your peace
        and presence.
Give me
  a renewed hope
    in the midst
      of my despair.

I waited patiently for God to help me; then he listened and heard my cry. He lifted me out of the pit of despair, out from the bog and the mire, and set my feet on a hard, firm path and steadied me as I walked along. He has given me a new song to sing, of praises to our God. Now many will hear of the glorious things he did for me, and stand in awe before the Lord, and put their trust in him. Many blessings are given to those who trust the Lord, and have no confidence in those who are proud, or who trust in idols. *Psalm 40:1-4*

But O my soul, don't be discouraged. Don't be upset. Expect God to act! For I know that I shall again have plenty of reason to praise him for all that he will do. He is my help! He is my God! *Psalm 42:11*

But happy is the man who has the God of Jacob as his helper, whose hope is in the Lord his God—the God who made both earth and heaven, the seas and everything in them. He is the God who keeps every promise, and gives justice to the poor and oppressed, and food to the hungry. He frees the prisoners, and opens the eyes of the blind; he lifts the burdens from those bent down beneath their loads. For the Lord loves good men. *Psalm 146:5-8*

MAIL CALL

Mail call brought me
　some letters today, Lord.
It was good to hear
　from my family
　　and friends.
I am grateful
　for their caring
　　and concern
　about my welfare
　　and well-being.
But I am concerned
　about their problems
　　and their difficulties.
Help us, Lord,
　to understand each other
　　and to be concerned
　　　about each other's needs,
　to show love
　　even when the going gets tough
　　　and no matter what it costs.
Thank you, God,
　for those who
　　remembered and
　for those who
　　took time to write.

Love is very patient and kind, never jealous or envious, never boastful or proud, never haughty or selfish or rude. Love does not demand its own way. It is not irritable or touchy. It does not hold grudges and will hardly even notice when others do it wrong. It is never glad about injustice, but rejoices whenever truth wins out. If you love someone you will be loyal to him no matter what the cost. You will always believe in him, always expect the best of him, and always stand your ground in defending him. *1 Corinthians 13:4-7*

Who makes a mistake and I do not feel his sadness? Who falls without my longing to help him? Who is spiritually hurt without my fury rising against the one who hurt him? *2 Corinthians 11:29*

If you will humble yourselves under the mighty hand of God, in his good time he will lift you up. *1 Peter 5:6*

MEALTIME

Mealtime is
 a drag, Lord.
The dining hall—
 the noise,
  the confusion,
   the griping
 hardly make for
  a good atmosphere
   for eating.
The food
 is not that good
 and my appetite
 is not that great.
O Lord,
 help me to be grateful
  for what I get
   be it too much
    or too little;
 help me to appreciate
  the food I have
   so I don't have
    to go hungry.
Just give me
 a better appetite
  to enjoy it.

For everything God made is good, and we may eat it gladly if we are thankful for it, and if we ask God to bless it, for it is made good by the Word of God and prayer. *1 Timothy 4:4, 5*

So my counsel is: Don't worry about *things*—food, drink, and clothes. For you already have life and a body—and they are far more important than what to eat and wear. Look at the birds! They don't worry about what to eat— they don't need to sow or reap or store up food—for your heavenly Father feeds them. And you are far more valuable to him than they are. Will all your worries add a single moment to your life? *Matthew 6:25-27*

A wise man is hungry for truth, while the mocker feeds on trash.

When a man is gloomy, everything seems to go wrong; when he is cheerful, everything seems right!

It is better to eat soup with someone you love than steak with someone you hate. *Proverbs 15:14, 15, 17*

NIGHT

I am alone, God;
   the lights
     have been put out,
   the cell doors
     have all been locked,
   the corridors
     have grown empty and still.
And I am alone—
   the long night hours
     are before me;
   the shouting and cursing
     echo through
       the cells;
   the darkness
     exaggerates my fears
     and worries.
It is difficult to sleep
   but more difficult
     to stay awake.
O God, I am alone.
   As I lay down
     to sleep,
       help me
     to feel
       your presence.

He will take care of the helpless and poor when they cry to him; for they have no one else to defend them. He feels pity for the weak and needy, and will rescue them. He will save them from oppression and from violence, for their lives are precious to him. *Psalm 72:12-14*

I will lie down in peace and sleep, for though I am alone, O Lord, you will keep me safe. *Psalm 4:8*

Have two goals: wisdom—that is, knowing and doing right—and common sense. Don't let them slip away, for they fill you with living energy, and are a feather in your cap. They keep you safe from defeat and disaster and from stumbling off the trail. With them on guard you can sleep without fear; you need not be afraid of disaster or the plots of wicked men, for the Lord is with you; he protects you. *Proverbs 3:21-26*

DOUBT

O God,
 in the bleakness
  and barrenness
 of this place,
  how can I know
   you exist;
    you are real?
I've been told
 that you are the Creator-God.
  Did you create such a
   hell-hole as this?
I've been told
 that you are the Savior-God.
  Can you save such
   lost souls as these?
I've been told
 that you are the Comforting-God.
  Can your Spirit bring peace
   to the disturbed prisoners
    in this place?
O God,
 I have my doubts
  that you are real
 otherwise why can't
  I believe and know
   you are here
    with me?

The Spirit of the Lord is upon me; he has appointed me to preach Good News to the poor; he has sent me to heal the brokenhearted and to announce that captives shall be released and the blind shall see, that the downtrodden shall be freed from their oppressors, and that God is ready to give blessings to all who come to him. *Luke 4:18, 19*

O Lord, you have examined my heart and know everything about me. You know when I sit or stand. When far away you know my every thought. You chart the path ahead of me, and tell me where to stop and rest. Every moment, you know where I am. You know what I am going to say before I even say it. You both precede and follow me, and place your hand of blessing on my head.

This is too glorious, too wonderful to believe! I can *never* be lost to your Spirit! I can *never* get away from my God! If I go up to heaven, you are there; if I go down to the place of the dead, you are there. If I ride the morning winds to the farthest oceans, even there your hand will guide me, your strength will support me. If I try to hide in the darkness, the night becomes light around me. For even darkness cannot hide from God; to you the night shines as bright as day. Darkness and light are both alike to you. *Psalm 139:1-12*

REPENTANCE

Lord,
   I have come to see myself
     as you see me:
   I am lost
     and I need to be found;
   I am empty
     and I need to be filled;
   I am sinful
     and I need to be cleansed;
   I am dead
     and I need to be born again.
O God,
   I confess that I
     have disobeyed your will;
     have neglected your teachings;
     have rejected your love;
     have denied your truth.
Lord, turn my life around,
   help me to give up
     my sinful ways;
   put a new mind
     and a new heart
       within me;
   give me the fulness of life
     you have promised
       to all who come to you.

Jesus replied, "With all the earnestness I possess I tell you this: Unless you are born again, you can never get into the Kingdom of God." *John 3:3*

And so, dear brothers, I plead with you to give your bodies to God. Let them be a living sacrifice, holy—the kind he can accept. When you think of what he has done for you, is this too much to ask? *Romans 12:1*

I will give them hearts that respond to me. They shall be my people and I will be their God, for they shall return to me with great joy. *Jeremiah 24:7*

And I will give you a new heart—I will give you new and right desires—and put a new spirit within you. I will take out your stony hearts of sin and give you new hearts of love. And I will put my Spirit within you so that you will obey my laws and do whatever I command. *Ezekiel 36:26, 27*

The thief's purpose is to steal, kill and destroy. My purpose is to give life in all its fullness. *John 10:10*

FORGIVENESS

Lord God,
 I stand before you
  as a condemned prisoner
   fully accepting
    the consequences
     of my crime.
I need
 to be forgiven, Lord—
  forgiven by you,
   by those I wronged,
    by society.
I don't know
 where to begin or
 how to begin or
 with whom to begin.
But Lord,
 I pray that I may
  first find forgiveness
   with you.
Forgive me
 of the crimes
  I have committed
 against you and
  my fellowman.
Give me a
 clear conscience and
  grant me
  your peace.

But if we are living in the light of God's presence, just as Christ does, then we have wonderful fellowship and joy with each other, and the blood of Jesus his Son cleanses us from every sin.

If we say that we have no sin, we are only fooling ourselves, and refusing to accept the truth. But if we confess our sins to him, he can be depended on to forgive us and to cleanse us from every wrong. [And it is perfectly proper for God to do this for us because Christ died to wash away our sins.] *1 John 1:7-9*

Come, let's talk this over! says the Lord; no matter how deep the stain of your sins, I can take it out and make you as clean as freshly fallen snow. Even if you are stained as red as crimson, I can make you white as wool! *Isaiah 1:18*

He is merciful and tender toward those who don't deserve it; he is slow to get angry and full of kindness and love. He never bears a grudge, nor remains angry forever. He has not punished us as we deserve for all our sins, for his mercy toward those who fear and honor him is as great as the height of the heavens above the earth. He has removed our sins as far away from us as the east is from the west. He is like a father to us, tender and sympathetic to those who reverence him. *Psalm 103:8-13*

FAITH

My God,
  you have come to me
    in my forsakenness;
  you have consoled me
    in my loneliness;
  you have cleansed me
    from my guiltiness;
  you have changed me
    from my sinfulness.
Lord,
  you have become
    real to me:
  I can call you
    "my Lord and my God";
  I can claim your victory
    in my life.
Help me, God—
  help me to grow
    in my faith in you;
  help me to trust you
    now in the present
      and with my future;
  help me to share my faith
    with those around me
      so they, too, may know
      the new life you have
        for them.

For salvation that comes from trusting Christ—which is what we preach—is already within easy reach of each of us; in fact, it is as near as our own hearts and mouths. For if you tell others with your own mouth that Jesus Christ is your Lord, and believe in your own heart that God has raised him from the dead, you will be saved. For it is by believing in his heart that a man becomes right with God; and with his mouth he tells others of his faith, confirming his salvation. *Romans 10:8-10*

How we thank God for all of this! It is he who makes us victorious through Jesus Christ our Lord!

So, my dear brothers, since future victory is sure, be strong and steady, always abounding in the Lord's work, for you know that nothing you do for the Lord is ever wasted as it would be if there were no resurrection. *1 Corinthians 15:57, 58*

Because of his kindness you have been saved through trusting Christ. And even trusting is not of yourselves; it too is a gift from God. Salvation is not a reward for the good we have done, so none of us can take any credit for it. It is God himself who has made us what we are and given us new lives from Christ Jesus; and long ages ago he planned that we should spend these lives in helping others. *Ephesians 2:8-10*

FREEDOM

Lord,
   I have been imprisoned
      by myself and my sinfulness;
      by society and its laws;
      by the walls and doors
         of this prison.
But God,
   today I thank you
      for setting me free
      for giving me new freedom
         which no walls
            or systems or people
         can take away
            or deny me.
Lord,
   enable me to use
   my new-found freedom
   to help set others free;
   to let them know
      you can break the chains
         that bind them;
      you can set at liberty
         those who are in prison;
      you can give freedom to
         those who are in bondage
            to themselves
            to others
            to society.

If the Lord calls you, and you are a slave, remember that Christ has set you free from the awful power of sin; and if he has called you and you are free, remember that you are now a slave of Christ. You have been bought and paid for by Christ, so you belong to him—be free now from all these earthly prides and fears. *1 Corinthians 7:22, 23*

In those days when you were slaves of sin you didn't bother much with goodness. And what was the result? Evidently not good, since you are ashamed now even to think about those things you used to do, for all of them end in eternal doom. But now you are free from the power of sin and are slaves of God, and his benefits to you include holiness and everlasting life. For the wages of sin is death, but the free gift of God is eternal life through Jesus Christ our Lord. *Romans 6:20-23*

So if the Son sets you free, you will indeed be free. *John 8:36*

PRAISE

My heart is
  full of praise, Lord—
  full of praise for
    reaching down to me and
    revealing yourself to me
      in this dreadful place.
Thank you, God,
  for your love
    which knows no limits;
  for your grace
    which erases all guilt;
  for your forgiveness
    which gives perfect freedom;
  for your salvation
    which brings new life.
Thanks, too, God,
  for seeing me through
    difficult days;
  for giving me courage to
    face ridicule and hostility;
  for granting me a new lease on life
    at a time when I faced
      only darkness and despair.
I praise you, Lord,
  for your holy presence
    in this place and
    in my life.

I bless the holy name of God with all my heart. Yes, I will bless the Lord and not forget the glorious things he does for me.

He forgives all my sins. He heals me. He ransoms me from hell. He surrounds me with lovingkindness and tender mercies. He fills my life with good things! My youth is renewed like the eagle's! He gives justice to all who are treated unfairly. *Psalm 103:1-6*

Oh, praise the Lord, for he has listened to my pleadings! He is my strength, my shield from every danger. I trusted in him, and he helped me. Joy rises in my heart until I burst out in songs of praise to him. *Psalm 28:6, 7*

Hallelujah! I want to express publicly before his people my heartfelt thanks to God for his mighty miracles. All who are thankful should ponder them with me. For his miracles demonstrate his honor, majesty, and eternal goodness.

Who can forget the wonders he performs—deeds of mercy and of grace? *Psalm 111:1-4*

And out of the throne came a voice that said, "Praise our God, all you his servants, small and great, who fear him."

Then I heard again what sounded like the shouting of a huge crowd, or like the waves of a hundred oceans crashing on the shore, or like the

mighty rolling of great thunder, "Praise the Lord. For the Lord our God, the Almighty, reigns...."
Revelation 19:5, 6